UBER @ 2 AM

Bill Powers

UBER @ 2 AM

by Bill Powers

Book layout by Laura Ashton
laura@gitflorida.com

Cover photograph by Bill Powers
Author's photo, p.83, from the author.

Disclaimer

The stories are just as they happened – they're true.
However, all the riders' names have been changed
... and *sometimes* you may run into some *mildly* offensive language.

ISBN: 979-8394819216

Printed in the United States of America

Dedication

*This book is dedicated to the man who taught me what is right,
what is wrong, and most importantly, a sense of humor,
even when I don't feel like laughing ...*

James K Powers
July 7, 1917 – December 25, 1975

Thanks for the lessons, Dad.

Table of Contents

Table of Contents, cont.

Dear Reader,

Thank you for purchasing my first book. I hope you enjoy the read. If you were not able to attend any of my book signings at many of the restaurants and bars mentioned in the book, please consider this your signed copy!

Drive safely, and always call one of us if you have had one too many.

Sincerely,

Introduction

My father was killed by a drunk driver on Christmas Eve 1975. And he predicted his death.

Great way to start a book of funny stories, right? Actually, if there is an afterlife, I just put a big smile on my father's face.

So, if you want to skip the rest of the introduction and get right to my outlandish but true stories, please do so. You might find your way back here to understand some of my actions. More details are revealed at the end of this book.

Back to my dad. First, he was a happy guy. He was unflappable. Nothing surprised him. My sister and I got to know him slowly as he started hanging around the house years after our mom and our biological dad divorced. We became latch key kids before that term was invented. At some point, he had magically moved in with us. A few years later, he adopted us. Our name changed and we became a happy family.

He influenced me in so many ways, but the overriding lesson was, "You've got to have a sense of humor." He told me numerous times to realize when bad things happen, even catastrophic events, in time something is going to strike you as funny about it.

My mother was very religious. She would drag my sister and me to the United Methodist church at Central Avenue and Missouri in northeast Phoenix. I would drag my feet and yell, "Forced religion," and looking at my dad reading his newspaper, "How come he doesn't have to go?" I'd scream. My dad would pull me aside later and explain, "Your mother and I came to an agreement before we got married. She has her religion, and I have my *Higher Power*. We have compromised, and I have agreed to attend her church twice a year: Easter and Christmas Eve candle lighting." Any raised eyebrows yet?

He would always end up by saying, "Your mother's religion will be the death of me yet." He said that in jest many times. I learned the

7

hard way that mantras can be bad as well as good.

And that brings us right up to 1975, and the horrible Christmas Day that followed. My jobs that morning were identifying my dad's mangled body, and driving to my grandparents to inform them their only son was killed. Not so merry.

All valley police agencies searched for the hit and run driver's white Mustang, and an off-duty Phoenix cop found it one week after the 19-year-old previously convicted alcohol and drug addict killed my dad coming out of my mother's church on Christmas Eve.

So, after almost fifty years in an exciting industry with numerous positions and global travel, I retired. I started playing tennis, not enjoying horrible golf, and hanging around a few bars too frequently. At lunch one day, a couple of longtime friends suggested driving for UBER, as they were doing, and my ego immediately kicked in with, "What, after decades in a prestigious position, I am going to become a cab driver?" They explained it was nothing like that. I would be driving my own car, choosing when and if I wanted to work, and I could continue to enjoy meeting new and interesting people. That was almost seven years ago, and I am glad I did. Other Uber drivers think I am crazy for choosing to drive weekend nights picking up drunks to get them home safely without killing anyone. Do I have to explain it?

So, sit back, imagine you are riding along in a mid-sized SUV through the streets and highways of the Valley of the Sun, at 2 a.m., bring your sense of humor and enjoy the trip.

– Bill

1 ~ Girl on a Rock

2:10 AM – Sunday morning

Cave Creek is a town just north of Phoenix that celebrates dark skies at night, so there are very few streetlamps. Coupled with no serious zoning regulations on address signs, finding a particular house sometimes requires a spotlight and a slow speed. I was in the process of locating a house and I heard a timid voice ask, "Are you the UBER driver?" My spotlight found a young lady in a short black cocktail dress sitting on a boulder between two houses.

I slowed to stop and open the door for her when she shouted, "No, keep going! I'll tell you when to stop." Puzzled, I continued to creep along the deserted residential street, with my rider attempting to keep up in 4-inch heels on the gravel path alongside the roadway, constantly looking back at the house. After travelling about 200 feet, she called out, "Okay, this should be far enough."

She hopped in directly behind the driver's seat, and I first asked her name, as it wasn't the male name highlighted on my screen. "Oh, that's my friend's name. He's paying my fare. I'm Annie."

I replied, "I'm Bill, your driver, and do you mind explaining what that walking was about?"

Annie quipped, "Well, I was a *very* bad girl tonight."

My response was, "Do tell."

She started on a version of her exploits during the evening with, "I was sleeping with a married guy." Being that it was still considered Saturday night, I mentioned that there were probably millions of women doing the same thing. She said, "Probably, but they weren't married to an executive of Ring Technologies." I understood the reference and asked how she passed by the video doorbell without setting off its automatic phone notification to the owner.

"Oh, he held his hand over it. He then told me to sidle down the face of the house and pointed out the boulder between houses that was out of view from the additional cameras that were installed on the house."

Hmm ... seems like this was not the first time he has done this. I didn't say anything.

As I started our 25-minute trip to her place, she started Facetiming girlfriends to recount the evening's festivities. She started with Julie and described a robust PG-rated accounting of their lovemaking, ending the call by saying, "Say hi to my UBER driver, Bill," and stuck her phone through the space between the front seats. I dutifully waved back.

Karen was her second call—*Are all these friends actually awake and waiting for these 2 a.m. calls?*—and Annie started amplifying the night's festivities. I had to award that version a solid R-rating. Quite colorful. As before, her hand shot through the gap and she again said, "Say hi to my UBER driver, Bill." I waved again.

I heard some mumbling, her seat belt unfastening and as she climbed through between the seats and deposited herself in the passenger seat. *Did I mention her short black cocktail dress?* She announced, "Well, you don't seem to be a rapist." *Yikes!* I told her to buckle her seat belt.

She then called her third girlfriend, Gretchen, and this version of the night was straight out of *Fifty Shades of Gray* including sex swings, bondage, blindfolds, and handcuffs. *Does she realize that I have heard every escalating version? It probably was not lost on her.* After relating this new X-rated version of the night, she added the introduction of her UBER driver and I again waved back.

Gretchen announced, "Annie, pick up now," to which my rider put the phone to her ear and started giggling. She ended the call with, "Okay, I'll tell him." My obvious response was, "Tell me what?" Annie looked at me and said, "Gretchen said that I should dump the married guy and screw my UBER driver!."

Shit. Now what? Did I mention she was as cute as a button, and dressed to the nines? Nope, I might have omitted that part.

I looked at her and said, "There are two reasons that it's not going to happen." Raising my left hand and wiggling my ring finger, I said, "One, I am obviously more married than the guy you were just with.

And two, I have a granddaughter about your age, so I must respectfully decline." *Yikes, did I just do that? That surprised the heck out of me.*

So, what did Annie do for the rest of the 6 minutes left of our journey? She folded her arms over her chest and pouted ... the whole way. No words were spoken. When I pulled up in front of her apartment complex, she got out, walked around the front of my car, and rapped on my window. I rolled it down, she leaned in and whispered, "Are you sure that you don't want to come up for a glass of wine and see what might happen?"

My reply was, "Annie, I would absolutely LOVE to come upstairs with you, but the ramifications of that action are too horrible to contemplate. Divorce, losing all my money, my home, my car and just about everything." She turned around, sashayed away, flipping up her skirt in the process—ensuring I noted her lack of underwear, in case I missed it when she was climbing between the seats—and said, "Well, you don't know what you are missing." She was wrong about that. I knew what I was missing. I had already weighed the pros and cons. Damn it, the cons won out. *How did I get here? Knowledge. Old age. Shit.*

Next morning, as is her habit every now and then, my wife innocently asked, "Did anything crazy happen last night?" I had already pulled the chip out of my interior / exterior dash cam and put it in my desktop computer. I told her to sit down, I would go get her a cup of coffee and I hit play. I took my time making her coffee and returned just as the clip ended.

She appeared flushed, and said with a straight face, "Damn, that girl was cute. I think I might have done her."

We have been together way too long for me to take the bait. She wanted me to act incredulous, and bluster that she should be grateful her husband was so loyal. *Devious woman.* I just smiled knowing that I dodged a bullet with the aid of an all-telling video.

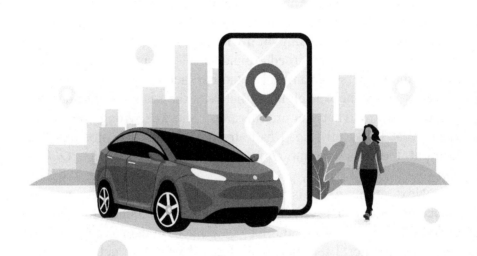

2 ~ Sonny & Cher

2:20 AM – Saturday morning

I accepted a request to pick up someone named Rick, at a bar named Club Volt. I was not familiar with the bar, but the street intersection was in north Phoenix and familiar to me. I pulled up to a dark parking lot with the building in back. I texted Rick that I had arrived, got out of my car, opened the rear car door, and waited for him to emerge. The bar door opened and a blond "Cher" walked out holding hands with a Sonny clone. As they approached, I stuck my hand out, looked at Sonny and said, "You must be Rick." A booming James Earl Jones baritone voice boomed, "No ... I am!"—out of the statuesque 6-foot blonde. I think I recovered quickly enough and replied, "Sorry, my mistake," and we started our 18-minute drive to a Melrose District address.

My curiosity and very poor ability to keep my mouth shut got the better of me when I asked Rick, "May I ask you a personal question?" —to which Sonny started all kinds of snorting noises. Rick very nicely replied, "Sure. What's up?"

"Well, you appear to be a very distinguished looking woman in an incredibly form fitting miniskirt. Where do hide your junk?" Sonny started snorting again, but Rick hushed him up saying, "There are special forms of underwear that have pouches that you put your penis in. They have Velcro straps that thread between your legs and a corresponding attachment patch on the rear waistband. You can cinch it up nice and tight and no one can tell. They are called Manties."

I asked where he purchased them and he said, "I used to buy them at Fredrick's of Hollywood." I asked the obvious next question of where does he buy them now? Excitedly, he answered, "Amazon! They are a quarter of the price, and they arrive at my door in a brown non-descript package. It's great!"

When we arrived at their nice turn of the century cottage home, Rick invited me in because he loves talking to straight guys (Sonny snorted again), but I said I was still picking up people who weren't in the condition to drive and wished them the best.

PLEASE don't do what I did in an effort to fact-check the above story—Google or search Amazon for "Manties." It took months of ignoring outrageous advertisements for all kinds of alternative lifestyle products and services—oh God, the services—for them to finally die out.

3 ~ I Can Steer Better Than You

2:15 AM – Saturday morning

Have you ever met anyone that keeps getting more inebriated even after they quit drinking? I responded to a request from Sandbar Mexican Grille, an upscale large bar / restaurant in Desert Ridge Marketplace in north Phoenix. This kind of call usually means someone has been tossed out of the establishment for behavior issues. Most of the bouncers there are off-duty cops, and I have gotten to know a few. When I pulled up, one of them leaned in and said, "We 86'd these guys. They might be a little unruly. Good luck."

"And you're putting them in *my* car? Thanks a lot!"

"Don't worry. I've already called in your license plate."

"What does that mean?" I said.

"We'll be keeping an eye out on your car. If you have any trouble, stop the car, grab your phone, exit the car, call 911 and we'll take it from there."

Armed with that encouraging intelligence, they piled into my SUV, three in the back, and my "client" Steve in the passenger seat for the 30 minute plus adventure. I dropped them off one at a time, until all that was left was Steve, who had become more effusive and louder as the trip had progressed.

We were about 2 minutes from his home. He wasn't aware, but this is a route I travel numerous times per day. I live about two miles north of where this near disaster occurred. We were traveling north on Tatum Blvd, a 4-lane street with xeriscape landscaped median and sides. I was slowing down from the 45mph limit, and I had turned on my signal in preparation for a right turn coming up on Ranger Drive when Steve exclaimed, "You are going to miss my turn!" and reached over, grabbed the wheel, and yanked his left hand down.

As I slammed on the brakes, I instinctively hit the back of his hand with a closed fist hard very hard. He retracted his hand and screamed "That hurts! What did you do that for?" When he screamed and let go of the wheel, I was able to yank the wheel the other way to miss the objects hurtling toward us. We had just come to rest after jumping the curb, skidding across the meandering sidewalk, dodging a large Palo Verde tree and stopping two feet away from a six-foot block wall leading into a back yard probably featuring one of the hundreds of pools in the area.

I gestured outside the car and asked him to see where we were due to his physical assault on my steering wheel. I shut the engine off, pulled my keys, got out of the car, and walked around my vehicle to see if the tires or rims were damaged. Amazingly, they appeared okay. I got back in the car and yelled, "You jerk. You almost got us killed!" I was furious and didn't hold back, "What the hell were you thinking?" Thinking back I realized what a stupid question that was. He was drunk and wasn't capable of thinking.

He looked down at his feet, shook his head sadly and stammered, "I ... I'm sorry man ... really sorry."

I could see he was sincere. I took a deep breath and let it out slowly. "Try that shit again and you will be spending the rest of this night in jail."

I am certain he woke up the next morning with a hand the size of a catcher's mitt and had no idea how that happened. Needless to say, I did not award him 5 stars.

I did file a report with UBER so he wouldn't pull that stunt with any other driver. I notified Uber that he might file a complaint against me for hitting his hand and offered to send them the footage from my dash cam. The response was "You did the right thing. We will defend your actions. If we receive a claim, we will request the video." They blackballed him and I never heard anything more.

4 ~ Stem Cell Research

12:15 AM – Sunday morning

Not all early morning pickups are drinking related. I receive a number of airport requests. Surprise, Arizona, is a very fast-growing bedroom community western suburb of Phoenix, in the Valley of the Sun. Homes are still affordable out that way, but they come with a longer commute. Quite a few people prefer the rideshare option when traveling into Phoenix proper.

I picked up a young man there and started our 35-minute drive to Sky Harbor. As usual, I asked him what he did for a living. "I am a stem cell researcher." I have been interested in that area of medical innovation, but I had noticed something had changed. I asked, "Why haven't I heard the far-right complaining that you guys were encouraging abortions by using fetal tissue?"

He chuckled and asked me how long ago that I had noticed all the noise going away. "I'm not sure, maybe a year and a half or so," I responded. This trip took place in 2020. He replied that my estimate was close, so I asked again what had changed. He smirked and said, "Our leadership finally got their heads out of their asses and decided to drop that unwinnable fight all together."

Knowing the incredible promise of the medical breakthroughs to be created from stem cell research, I asked what they are using now (instead of fetal membranes). "We are, and have been, using placental tissue that works every bit as well." he replied. Being that I am a father of three now-adult kids, I exclaimed, "Really. As I remember, the placentas were considered hospital waste when my three kids were born. I think I might have even seen disposal fees on my bill." He laughed and said that's not the case anymore. The research community is paying for healthy placentas now.

I got him to the airport in plenty of time and thanked him for his knowledge and his work. Who says that you can't keep learning when you are old?

5 ~ COVID, Moon and Foil Hats

2:21 AM – Saturday morning

The Alaskan Bush Company is a large restaurant / bar located on Grand Avenue, one of only two diagonal streets located in an otherwise perfectly laid out grid pattern that defines the City of Phoenix road system. To be fair to the large boulevard, it parallels the main railroad tracks on the western part of the city. That might also explain the fact that the Bush Company is mainly a topless bar probably due to its proximity to the tracks.

I pulled up to the main door as approximately forty guys were leaving—bars in Phoenix are required to stop selling alcohol at 2 a.m.— and I located my fare, Tony, and his buddy. This was post pandemic, so when they were getting in, I asked them if they had been vaccinated. *See my chapter entitled "Mask Nazi Not" for reference to my response this night.*

It was all Tony needed. He started in exclaiming, "This COVID nonsense is bullshit!" I immediately glanced at the time enroute number on the lower corner of the UBER screen praying silently that it wasn't 20 minutes or more. It cooperated with a livable 8 minutes, and I just kept driving. Tony continued, "Nobody has died from COVID. They are dying from pneumonia, black lung disease, the flu and old age. This is all hopped up crap from big pharma and greedy politicians. Doctors are all in on the scam to get more money for their hospitals by inflating the death toll attributed to COVID."

I honestly lost track of all the sub plots he espoused. *Why do I get all the nuts?* I just kept my mouth shut, and curiously so did his friend.

He started winding down at 4 minutes to go, and I had a fleeting thought that we might have a quiet ride the rest of the way when Tony shouted, "And another thing. Man has never landed on the moon! It was

19

all a Hollywood sham. It was filmed in the Nevada desert at Area 51. Steven Spielberg directed the whole thing. They made him sign a massive non-disclosure agreement which keeps him from talking to this day." *Really crazy.* This topic kept him talking for another two long minutes. Two more to go.

"And another thing," he blurted. "Aluminum foil damn sure repels the gamma rays that the government has been raining down on its populace. But it is important that the foil must cover the entire backside of your head."

Apparently looking at half clothed females seems to offer some additional protection because I couldn't detect any metal under his cowboy hat.

We finally arrived at their mobile home not far from the aforementioned railroad tracks. His buddy jumped out of the car without ever muttering a word, and as much as I kept reminding myself never argue with a fanatic, I said to Tony, "Isn't it great that we can live in a country where everyone is entitled to their own beliefs?"—*purposely omitting the words 'bat shit crazy' from my question.* He stopped for a second, leaned in and pointing his finger at me and said, "I knew YOU would understand."

I smiled, waved back, drove one block south, turned left and parked because I was doubled over in laughter. As I was wiping away the tears from my eyes, I thought, who says UBER'ing can't be fun?

6 ~ Not So Silent Zippers

12:30 AM – Sunday morning

The Blue Martini is an upscale nightclub on High Street in north Phoenix that caters to twenty-something movers and shakers. It is a great place to meet new lovers. I picked up two of the very pretty people who were in a very romantic embrace. I had to wait for the bouncer to separate them long enough to indicate their ride was here. He and I shared a knowing look. "Good luck with these two. We had to toss them out of the restaurant because of other customers complaining."

My customer was Brad. It became obvious they just wanted to get to one of their homes as soon as possible. They had obviously been drinking heavily and only had one thing on their mind. "I will get you home quickly," I assured them. I was answered by silence from the back seat. That is until I heard seat belts unclicking and the very distinct sound of zippers sliding one way or the other. I mentioned—as if anyone was listening to me—"I would prefer you guys would stay belted in."

Right. Those darn seat belts would only get in the way.

Well, it was during my first year of driving, and I figured this has happened to other drivers before, so I just continued driving. The ETA showed less than 10 minutes, but it seemed a whole lot longer of a drive. The not so muffled sounds of lovemaking continued until we were approaching their destination. I sounded like Al McCoy (the local Phoenix Sun's announcer) when I loudly called out, "Two minutes!" I heard the reverse sliding of zippers, and finally heard the snap of the seat belts back in place.

When I pulled up in front of an impressive condo, Brad smiled sheepishly, handed me a ten and said thanks for one of the best UBER rides he had ever enjoyed.

I quit driving for the night and had my interior detailed the next day. The ten didn't come close to covering the bill.

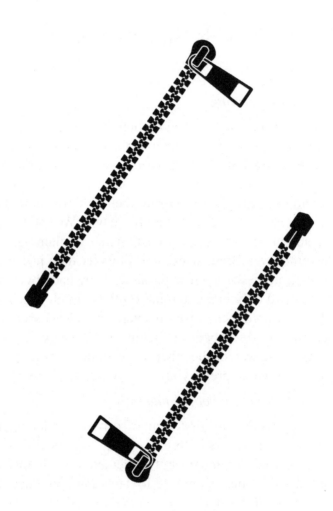

7 ~ Desert Rapist Attack

11:40 PM – Friday night

Across from the Blue Martini on High Street, is a more moderately priced restaurant called Mellow Mushroom Pizza. This particular location sports a well-stocked bar, and based on the number of very drunk people that I have picked up there, some very heavy-handed bartenders as well.

So, it didn't surprise me when I had to help a friend of my rider, Margaret, to my car. One of the other patrons helped me get her into my back seat. She was mumbling, but not very coherent. I asked Margaret if she wanted to call paramedics, but she insisted that her friend was okay. She just had too much to drink. I managed to belt her into the rear, and she immediately slumped over and started snoring.

Margaret jumped into the passenger seat and started giving me a synopsis of their exciting day in Phoenix. They were both from Chicago, and this was mid-January. They couldn't believe they were walking around in shirtsleeves and actually tanning their faces. They skipped some of the convention meetings and UBERed around town. Obviously, they were imbibing constantly enjoying the local liqueurs. *It's amazing how many cactus drinks exist here in Arizona.*

As we were chatting, I was taking them to a nearby Holiday Inn Express located adjacent to Loop 101 and Tatum Blvd. It shares a strange entrance with the adjoining Cambria Hotel. The approaching road splits between an office complex and a food strip center and ends in a tee. Looking straight out the window, Margaret saw nothing but desert for miles.

Instantly, her inebriated brain shouted WARNING, and her Chicago roots jumped into gear. "Rapist!" she yelled. "You are not going to drive us into the desert and molest us!" Whereupon she started hitting me with her purse and screaming at the top of her lungs. I fended off the blows and shouted, "Quit hitting me! What the hell is wrong with you? Just look left, dammit!"

She looked past my fetal positioned body and saw the familiar green and white Holiday Inn logo. Thankfully, the purse which had to have weighed 20 pounds, quit coming down on my head, and she started apologizing. "Oh, I am so sorry. I just saw nothing but open desert, and I thought you were going to have your way with us!" *Christ. Really?*

Her apologies continued all the way to the hotel entrance, where I went in and asked for assistance to get her friend—who never woke up during the screaming—out of my back seat. With the aid of the hotel employee, we poured her friend into their hotel room.

She continued to beg for forgiveness as she shoved forty bucks into my hand. She said, "Please don't give me less than five stars."

Oh really? That was what concerned her? I was thinking more like she should be thanking me for not filing assault charges. Man, I had a headache for hours. Oh well.

8 ~ Bachelorette Party

11:00 PM – Thursday night

Piling five semi drunk girls into a mid-sized SUV is probably not the safest thing in the world, but when the two skinniest ones actually fit into one shoulder belt, it was tough to say no. They started at one place and continued bar hopping through old town Scottsdale. There are bars on every corner in that part of town, so it was more a problem of finding a place to park while waiting for them to emerge, than actually dropping them off. Thank God it was a Thursday, because the weekend crush would have prevented any of this partying. The small two-lane streets are completely clogged with drunk revelers Friday and Saturday nights. Every time we would arrive at one bar, they would extend the trip by adding stops through the UBER app, so they always had me ready for the next leg.

I got to know the entire bride's side of the wedding party. The event was coming up that Saturday afternoon. They were intent on getting the bride as intoxicated as possible before then.

Bachelor parties are truly less stressful. Strippers are a lot more laid back than these bridesmaids.

I made sure that everyone knew which seat pockets held the barf bags. "Please throw up outside my car!" I pleaded. Fortunately, the girls who needed them used the restrooms at the bars instead.

I got all of the girls back to their respective homes, and thought it was the end of my association with them. All in all, it was a fun Thursday night.

I Lost my Discover Card!

I received a call from the maid of honor. About two years into driving, I realized that UBER's lost and found procedures were less than effective, so I printed "Lost" cards with my cell number that I hand out to all riders so if someone thinks they left something in my car, they can call and check. I have returned quite a few articles over the years.

She had been calling all the bars, and no one had found it. I was her last chance. "Where were you sitting in my car?" I asked. She informed me that she was sitting on the other girl behind the passenger seat. *How did I forget that sight?*

I told her I hadn't seen it, but I would go look for her. Armed with a small flashlight, and ready to stand on my head, I went looking. After about 5 minutes of searching, I found it lodged deep in the seat sides where it could have remained hidden for months. I called her back and offered to bring it to her home, but she said the wedding party was all staying at the JW Marriot Resort near Desert Ridge, and could I bring it there. Actually, my house is no more than two miles from there and we set a time to meet in the lobby.

Imagine my surprise when the entire group of girls greeted me when I walked in the door singing "For He's The Jolly Good Fellow" when I handed her the card. The resort staff actually joined in as well.

They were all still drunk. Now, I ask you. Who says being an UBER driver can't be fun?

9 ~ Vomit Expense

1:50 AM - Sunday morning

One of the most often asked questions I receive from my nighttime riders is, "Has anyone ever thrown up in your car?." Heck, I ask the same question when I am a rider in other UBER drivers' cars. What's funny, is my answer and theirs is always the same. "Once." It's funny that all of us have had to learn the hard way the absolute signs of pending eruptions and have a set of plans already in place to avoid a mess in OUR CARS.

But first, let's get back to that one Sunday morning where I didn't plan well enough. I received a pickup request at a west side bar. I frankly have forgotten the name, but they are all the same. I will probably regret putting that remark in writing. The west side has a severe inferiority complex comparing themselves to the eastside and Scottsdale.

As I pulled up to the entrance, there was a serious fist fight in progress with bar patrons spilling out to observe. I did a quick check looking for my rider, Rick, but no one was paying attention to my lighted UBER sign and my emergency flashers, so I turned away from the brawl and headed out of the lot, just about to press the cancel button. I stopped when I saw four people waving at me near the entrance to the lot. When I approached them, Rick identified himself. I told them I was Bill, their driver, and invited them to get in. As always, I did a quick assessment. Two twenty-something, clean-cut guys, with two girls I would have carded in an instant if I was a bartender and not a lowly UBER driver.

The two guys seemed to be sober enough, but one of the two young girls looked a little green. Before we started moving, I gave them my pre-puke talk. Mainly, if any of them started feeling sick, they needed to let me know, and I would pull to the side of the road and let them open the door open and throw up on the ground. I explained the barf

27

bags were in the pockets in front of them. I actually gave them the cost warning as well. If anyone pukes in the car, Rick's card on file would be charged a lot of money. I had no idea what that charge was. I had been told it was substantial.

So, as we left for the 16-minute trek to one of the girl's addresses, two things became apparent. One, these guys had picked up the girls at the bar, poured drinks into them, and had amorous ideas. Two, the girls were extremely drunk and wanted nothing more than to get home safely. When I pulled up at the first girl's house, they both jumped out and ran to the door. They got in and apparently locked it. Probably smart.

I asked the guys what they wanted to do, and they said they would go to the door and the girls would eventually let them in. I seriously doubted that and noted several cars in the driveway. I was sure they were home safe.

I pointed that out to the obviously expectant suitors, and offered to drive them home, but they insisted on staying. "No, I am sure they will invite us in," Rick replied.

Oh well. Some other driver can take care of their retreat to their respective homes.

I didn't know that the youngest girl had decorated the back of my driver's seat until I picked up my next riders who asked if I knew someone had thrown up in the back seat. I apologized, got them to their location as soon as I could, and called it a night.

I took my car to the carwash the next morning and had them completely de-odorize and detail the entire interior. The cost was $150. I sent the bill along with photos and a synopsis of the event to UBER and chalked it up to the cost of driving for Uber. To my surprise, two days later, I received a credit to my account for the full amount. I have later learned UBER adds on an additional fee. I felt bad for Rick and his friend. I think that added insult to the disappointment they felt that night.

I wonder how the amorous guys got home. Oh well, I offered.

10 ~ Good Samaritans

Numerous weekend nights

Every UBER driver that actually cares about their riders develops "regulars." I have mentioned the Sandbar Mexican Grille in prior chapters. By day it is a decent local Mexican restaurant—we are a border state after all—but the night transforms it into a large meet (meat) market. There are two bars, inside and out, with its own sand beach under the patio.

I have picked up Mary and Bob there numerous times. They are a fun older couple that still love each other and enjoy going out most weekends. They are very outgoing and make friends easily. They like to sit at one of the bars and meet new people. I never know when I receive a pickup call from Bob if I am taking them home, or someone who they have met who have had too much alcohol, and they offer to have me drive them safely home. Hats off to the Bob and Marys of this world. That's why I feel they are true Good Samaritans.

The next two adventures are from Bob and Mary's acquaintances. They have truly saved a few people from themselves.

11 ~ Dead Dog Drinking

1:50 AM – Saturday morning

Bob stuck his head in my window and gave me a quick rundown on the seriously overweight mid-40s lady about to enter my back seat.

Stop. Don't hate me for that remark yet. My reason for the description will become apparent later.

Her dog had died earlier in the day, and she came to the bar to drown her sorrows. She drank enough to drown most of the patrons in the bar and was still standing … barely. Bob helped her into the back seat and away we went. I attempted to offer my condolences about the passing of her dog, but she immediately barked (pun intended), "You UBER drivers are idiots."

Ouch. That kinda stung.

I have learned the best action with a confrontational drunk is to simply say nothing. She continued her tirade with, "You put anybody in your car with no knowledge of their motives. It's the middle of the night for Christ sake! They could be killers, robbers, or molesters, and you are too stupid to realize it. For all you know, I could be a murderer!" With that statement, I heard her belt unclick, so I kept my eyes on her in the mirror. She leaned forward, raised her hand, and brought her fist down on my shoulder. *For a drunk woman, she packed a pretty hard punch. It hurt like Hell.*

I pulled over and calmly asked her to sit back, re-attach her seat belt, and I would get her home safely. When she did, I pulled back on the road and she started crying softly. I was starting to lose my sympathy for her dog passing.

We got to her gated community in Dove Valley at 2:20 a.m. and pulled up to the keypad. "What is your gate code?" I asked. Drunkenly, she replied, "Q ... A ... Z ..." I stopped her immediately. "No, I need four digits and if I need to add a pound sign in front or behind."

"Damn. I'm sorry. Hang on." She absolutely could not remember her code.

"Do you have it written down or stored in your phone?" She dug through her purse for some minutes. I heard the mobile key beeps and then she said, "I can't find my code," and began crying again. I was getting very tired of the crying.

Hmm. Two in the morning, a drunk woman who had threatened to kill me and called me stupid, crying in the back seat, and no cars going in our coming out. What to do?

I mentioned what I thought was a good idea, "There is a fire station up Cave Creek Road about one mile away. We can go there, and they can send a vehicle out with a universal gate opener."

Immediately after offering what I thought was a slick way out of our dilemma, she shrieked, "No firemen or police!" and really started wailing. The wailing was even worse than the crying. I took a breath and let it out slowly.

I knew she was a nut, and a very drunk one at that, but I couldn't stop myself. "Why not?"

She cried, "I am in the country illegally, and I will be deported."

Okay, I know all the politically correct nonsense about how we aren't supposed to profile people, but damn it, I am an UBER driver picking up people who get in my car, driving completely alone in the early morning very dark hours, so baloney to that. I had already missed the mark on this woman being a stabber. Now as I ran her appearance through my brain, I came up with, blonde, mid-forties Caucasian woman, certainly not a Mexican bone in her body, so I did it again.

I asked, "Where are you from?" She replied, "Canada."

I almost chuckled with the thought of all the abuse she would suffer at the hands of the Mounties.

I took a deep breath. "How long have you been here illegally?"

"Four years on a six-month visa," she replied.

Glancing around the gated community, and dusting off some fading real estate knowledge, I surmised that she either had to be independently wealthy, or she must be employed with a decent paying job.

In an effort to calm her down, I asked, "What do you do for a living?"

She said, "I am a school district supervisor."

Now, I have thrown all pre-conceived beliefs of the security of our school systems out the window.

"How did you keep working past your visa period?"

"No one asked," was her reply.

Ahh, Homeland Security, seriously take note. Okay, Bill, now what? Again, it is almost three in the morning. I'm still stuck with a very drunk moody illegal alien who pretended to stab me and call me an idiot in my car who doesn't seem to be going anywhere.

I offered, "You know, some of the gated subdivisions in this area have a pedestrian gate that is not locked." She came out of her crying jag and said, "Wait! We have one. It's behind that wall." She pointed directly in front of my car, about fifty feet away. I glanced at my screen and saw that her house was three lots in from the gate. "Do you think you can make it to your place?" I asked, seriously doubting her ability to do so.

"You bet," she slurred and, after a few minutes of opening the door, dropping her purse which spilled all over the pavement, picking up the mess, she shakily stood up and proceeded to walk a very uneven path to the break in the wall.

In retrospect, I should have taken off and left her to her own designs, but no. Not Bill the ethical UBER driver.

I sat watching her eventually traverse the 50 feet, step over the curb, and trip on the Safeguard security sign. Over she went, and my interior audio picked up my involuntary remark, "Shit!"

I flipped on my high beams, rolled the car up to the curb and got out to see if she was dead. My dash cam then picked up the silent movie that took place.

I went over and checked her out. She was flat on her back and had started crying again. I attempted to help her to her feet.

She had me by at least 100 pounds.

Now you understand my opening remarks at the beginning of this chapter.

It now was a hilarious silent movie. It recorded a few failed attempts to right her, one ending with both of us on our butts, and the successful one where I wedged my shoulder in her stomach area to anchor her to the block wall in between 18" pushups. When she was finally on her feet leaning against the thankfully well-constructed, very sturdy wall, I assessed where we were. I mentioned the thought of bringing some firefighters over to help her to get home, but that just started the wailing again. She pleaded with me, "I know I can make it to my house!"

In my previous career, I had been taught to constantly assess risk, so I told her I was still concerned for her safety. I said, "Look, since I can't get my car through the locked gate, I will let you attempt to walk home from here. However, you have my card. If you don't call or text me within the ten minutes to let me know you are safely in your house, I WILL call the fire department and ask them to do a welfare check on you. That might involve the police as well."

She assured me she would do just that, and I watched her detach herself from the wall and start heading in. Now, I did what I should have done earlier and headed back to pick up the bartenders and waitresses getting off work at the Sandbar.

About ten minutes later, I received the text "I made It!"

Thank you, God. If she would have fallen again, hit her head and bled out, I would be in hot water. I have watched enough crime shows to know the last person to see the dead person is guilty until proven innocent. That would just be my luck

12 ~ Back from Afghanistan

1:30 AM – Sunday morning

Good Samaritan Bob rapped on my window and told me a tale of my next rider. "This is a good kid." Bob explained. "Tom was a private in the army. He was on leave from his first middle east deployment and had poured his heart out as the bartenders kept pouring alcohol into him." Drinks mostly purchased by Bob, Mary and other grateful patrons at the bar thanking him for his service.

As Tom opened the door, I gave him my quick assessment review: early twenties, Caucasian, over 6'4", in shape, maybe 220lbs and extremely drunk.

He sat down, buckled in and immediately tried to lay down. He was hampered by the shoulder harness.

"Try using the center belt instead," I offered. He mumbled something that sounded like "Thanks," did as directed, and bam, he was out. I looked over my shoulder and saw that he took up all the back seat and then some. I revised my initial assessment. 6'7" at least.

Funny, just the size of my Marine son at his age. Nostalgia struck for a second.

I thanked Bob, and asked him if he realized how far away Tom lived, as I recognized the extreme west side valley area named Surprise that was keyed in. He said it was his honor to get Tom home safely.

Did I mention that I really respected Bob and Mary for their efforts?

I checked on Tom once again and started out on our projected 35-minute drive. My concern over my rider choking on any vomit laying down like that was lessened as I heard the snoring from the back seat. Nostalgia struck again and I started relaying funny stories about my son at his age to my comatose passenger.

Yes, I was talking to a passed-out kid in the back seat, but it pleased me. It reminded me of David McCallum's character "Ducky" in NCIS where, as the medical examiner, he routinely talks to his corpses.

The 35 minutes flew by, punctuated by sporadic loud snoring, and my running commentary. As we approached his mom's house, I started telling sleeping beauty that were almost there. Silence.

"Tom, time to wake up, buddy!"

Still only silence. I pulled up in front of the house and started trying to wake him. No luck. I tried all the *dad tricks* I learned with my kids. Yelling, shaking him, shaking him HARD, holding his nose and anything else I could think of. I finally got over my reluctance of waking mom, and anyone else that could help me get this very large kid out of my car. Despite ringing, knocking then pounding on both the front and side doors, no one answered.

Shit. I had been at it for almost ten minutes to no avail. I had checked his breathing, and actually felt for a pulse. He was alive, but in the deepest sleep I had ever seen. Double shit.

Finally, ready to duck the inevitable swing that I knew was coming, I opened my cold bottle of water and poured it on his forehead. *Success!* Up he came with murder in his eyes. I jumped back and was grateful for that seatbelt. When he got done cussing at me, I explained what had happened. What did he do? He laid his head back down and started to get comfortable again. *DAMN IT!*

"That's it," I yelled. "I am dialing 911 now and declaring you a drunk menace who won't get out of my car!" That finally registered and he started unwinding himself and stepped out of the car ... and fell straight forward. I tried to catch him, but once again I ended up on my butt with another rider. *And both of them were placed in my car by Bob and Mary. WTF?*

After we both struggled to our feet, I helped him to the side door. He found his key and stumbled through the door without a backward glance. I then started driving back into town, well past the time anyone else but me was out and about.

Shit. Oh well, just part of the job. I drove home feeling grateful that my son made it past those drinking binges just like I wished my rider the same. I slept well that night ... er, morning.

13 ~ Using the Dad Voice ~ White Ghetto Rap

11:45 PM – Saturday night

I was headed to an address in a very exclusive part of north Scottsdale. I had to pass through two gates with separate codes already provided by the rider, "Brad." When I drove up the drive, two young teenagers came dancing—no, seriously, actually dancing—out of the garage.

Again, my automatic assessment kicked in: White, very juvenile kids with expensive tennis shoes and gold jewelry hanging around their necks.

As they entered the back seat, I asked which one of them was Brad. They smaller of the two said Brad was "Daddyo."

Wait, that is out of the late fifties. Beatniks? Dobie Gillis? Maynard G Krebs? These kids in my back seat weren't even a thought in their parent's mind during that era. Has that made a comeback? I hoped not.

The keyed in destination was the center of at least 25 meet market establishments in old town Scottsdale. No way these kids were bar hopping. Any reasonable bouncer would card these juveniles.

I asked what the draw was there. "We lookin' for some hos," came out of one of them and he kicked on some very loud rap music on some audio device that I didn't see. Very loud. ***Strike ONE.***

They proceeded to regale me with all their accomplishments in the music industry. White pampered kids pretending to be rap gangsters. Every other word coming out of their mouths was either "fuck" or the previous "ho." ***Strike TWO.***

Then they started bragging about all the girls they had violated. Every one of their so-called conquests were named "Bitch", "Cunt", "Whore", and of course their oft too much used "Ho." That's it. ***Strike THREE.***

I pulled into a mall parking lot and stopped the car. I shut the engine off, and simply stared at them, not saying one word. They started looking at each other, then at me and started sweating. "Hey man. What the fuck?"

I didn't answer. I just kept glaring at them. "Hey, my dad's an attorney. He'll sue your ass." At that, I smiled and took my phone out of the holder.

UBER has a double-bind security system built on to all its apps. The driver and the user are prevented from seeing their respective numbers. However, there is a routine built in that will enable text and voice communication between parties. You simply click on the contact button and select between text and phone. It prompts, "Do you wish to call (rider's name)" and presents a Y/N button. The name Brad ("Daddyo") was clearly highlighted. I held my finger over the Y key and looked back.

"Now," I quietly stated, "You two tough guys have a couple choices.

"One, you turn that damn racket off. You sit staring straight ahead for the five minutes left of this ride, and you exit my car politely and most important of all, you keep your disgusting trash mouths shut."

"You have a second choice," I continued. "Keep that music blaring or say one more disrespectful word out of your mouths, I will hit send. I'll be more than happy to inform attorney 'Daddyo Brad' of your language and behavior in this car, and then I will dial 911 and declare I have two out of control punks in my car, and request assistance, which I know will be immediate, and probably involve handcuffs. Daddyo Brad can come and pick you two up at the Scottsdale Precinct jail.

"Okay gentlemen," I said. "What will it be, one or two? And think hard about how you indicate your very respectful choice to me." They turned off the god-awful noise, looked at each other and said, "Choice one please ... sir."

I put the phone back in the holder with the UBER app showing contact screen showing, not the normal GPS map. I knew where we were going. I wanted them to see Brad - Y/N for the balance of the trip. I didn't hear one more peep out of the now very timid little boys in the back.

They got out of the car at their destination, and actually thanked me for the ride. I wished them well with their endeavors, and added, "And remember, respect your elders."

I wondered how long they would stay quiet and respectful of others. Probably no longer than it took to walk into the first bar. Oh well.

As I drove away, I was hit with the sudden realization that I really had become my dad. Shit. Well, maybe not. Maybe they learned something.

14 ~ Reservation Woes

11:40 PM – Saturday night

I was headed for a gas station to fill up, but I had forgotten to go offline. The app beeped and announced a rider request not far from me. I clicked accept thinking it would be a short ride home for the rider. This was before UBER was informing us of the destination upfront. *Mistake ONE.*

The screen announced that the trip would take 39 minutes and the route was 28 miles long. I figured if I got close on gas, I would simply let the rider know that I needed to pull in a nearby station for a NASCAR type splash of fuel. No problem. *Mistake TWO.*

Again, the app only tells the driver of the final destination if you are gold status and above. It takes a new driver a while to reach that level, and I wasn't there yet, so I was kept in the dark. My rider, Sally, was pleasant and as I headed south on I-10 East, we started leaving Phoenix proper. *Mistake THREE.*

I kept glancing at the rapidly falling needle on the gauge and started sweating. I have lived in Arizona all my life. Phoenix is literally surrounded by reservations. If you have ever flown into Sky Harbor at night, you will notice very sharply defined areas of light and dark. Very dark.

I kept looking for gas stations, ANY gas station, to no avail. I was on the reservation headed to Sacaton. The town of Casa Grande was at least another 25 miles south, and we had traveled too far to turn around and head back to civilization.

The computer in my car said I had fuel for 8 miles more. The UBER app was reporting 10 miles to Sally's residence. I was using every gas saving technique I knew. Past midnight, running on fumes, no damn lights anywhere so I finally notified Sally of our predicament. First right thing I did. I hoped it wasn't too late.

"Sally, I have been running on fumes. I thought I would find a gas station and just throw a couple of gallons in so we wouldn't run out of gas. I think I made a mistake."

She tried to help. As we were approaching a dirt road that led to her house, she said, "Do you see that light way over there? It's a gas station about four miles down that dirt road. I think the pumps are credit card controlled and they work 24 hours a day. I haven't ever filled up there, but that is what I have been told." Shit. **Bill, you are a moron.**

As I pulled up to her mobile home, she ventured, "In case you run out, I think AAA will come out eventually."

Very comforting. I wondered which would show up first, the tow truck driver or sunrise.

I looked at my computer readout. No more miles were showing. The miles to go countdown had been replaced by a red "LOW FUEL" warning, *Double shit.*

I turned around and bumped along that dirt road at an incredibly slow pace for the four miles Sally had indicated, never taking my eyes off that very dim florescent light that turned out to be the only illumination for the ONE SINGLE PUMP beneath it. I rolled to a stop beside the pump, nervously looked for a credit card slot, and almost shouted for joy when I saw the Visa logo. The price per gallon was astronomical, but I really didn't care. I purposefully filled the tank hoping that every time I remembered what that tank cost me, it would remind me to never run that low on fuel again.

In a previous lifetime, I was a pilot for 30 years and a member of AOPA, Aircraft Owners and Pilots Association. They have a monthly magazine that went to all members. In the center of it was a regular story entitled "Never Again." It chronicled near death adventures that very intelligent and well-trained pilots found themselves in, and then breaks down everything that went wrong. It's never just one thing. It is a multitude of events piling up to create near disasters. The upbeat part of those stories was that the pilot did not crash, but made it down safely, hopefully much wiser for the event. I felt their embarrassment that night.

So, I dutifully reviewed the numerous errors I made.

1. I shouldn't have accepted the ride before filling the tank.
2. I picked up my rider and didn't immediately admit my error.
3. I should have asked the rider details of her destination.
4. I saw the distance and knew the gas level would become critical, but I kept driving.
5. I assumed there would be stations all along the route.

My flight instructor's voice came through loud and clear. "Not the best landing Powers, but at least you didn't break anything." The fact that I was headed home without spending the night on the reservation waiting for AAA was enough for me. Thank you, God.

15 ~ GPS Woes

Miscellaneous notes

Contrary to the belief of many, Global Positioning Systems are not perfect. The satellites are probably the strongest part of the system. Once they are in geosynchronous orbit and calibrated, they are pretty reliable. Getting the signal to your vehicle, having the strong enough reception to communicate with at least three of those, and surrounding terrain can screw the reliability up, but usually not for long.

The real glaring fault in the whole system is the old computer term GIGO—Garbage In, Garbage Out. At some point, every address had to be geocoded into the system. At some point in that process, a human being is involved.

A very little error at that point can result in big problems for delivery drivers, first responders, Tesla cars and UBER drivers. If garbage went in, garbage comes out. Let me share a couple of epic fails.

16 ~ Why Did Your House Move?

6:30 AM - Sunday morning

During the pandemic, after my doctor told me that based on my medical history (asthma, reduced lung capability and generally being old as dirt), if I contracted Covid (then called the Corona Virus) and was hospitalized, my odds of coming out alive were 50/50. The vaccine was just a vague promise at that point, so I stopped putting people in my car, and started doing UberEATS to reduce my exposure to the virus.

So, Sunday morning I had left the breakfast restaurant with a great smelling meal for two and followed the GPS instructions to an address in extreme north Scottsdale. I drove to the exact spot indicated on the app and started looking for the address listed. I drove slowly up and down the street, no luck. Most of the towns in the valley adhere to a long-established system of addressing properties. By looking at the numerical part of the full address, you can determine which side of the street the property is on. The suffix tells you the east / west component. It really is a very simple area to locate a specific house. Except when GIGO raises its ugly head. I pulled over and started walking up driveways to look for hidden address markers. Still, no luck.

There was a neighbor hand watering his lawn. *Yes, there are lawns in the desert, usually in front of houses owned by people who came from other climates.*

And don't get me started on all the trees and shrubs they have brought to the desert with them. Our once pristine air has now become one of the worst in the country for pollen pollution.

I walked up to him, introduced myself and asked if he knew where this particular address was. He said, "I don't recognize that number, but we have only been here for about a year. We moved here from Chicago." *My previous point just made.*

No one else was out and about, so my only course was to contact the customer through the app.

A nice woman answered, and I introduced myself and briefly described my dilemma. She asked, "Where are you now?" I gave her the cross streets, and she exclaimed, "Dear, you are about eight miles away from us." She went on to give me detailed instructions to their house, which I followed to the letter, and pulled up as she was coming out the door waving. I apologized for the delay, and she informed me this wasn't the first-time delivery drivers have been directed to the first place I had been at.

GIGO. I suggested that she add the closest cross streets in the comments section and add a note to ignore the GPS instructions, and that should cut down on the delivery issues.

I have seen those same instructions quite often. GIGO. Oh well.

17 ~ Oh, Rider, Where Art Thou?

6:45 PM - Friday evening

A request came in to pick up a rider named Susan at Arizona State University (ASU). Already, I could predict possible issues. ASU has grown to be one of the largest universities in the country, flying under the radar and quietly surpassing giants like Georgia State, the University of Texas, the University of Minnesota, Texas A&M and even Ohio State in total attendance. Tempe used to be a sleepy little university town. It has become a large part of the Valley of the Sun, especially after construction of Tempe Town Lake, a large man-made body of water constructed in the dry riverbed of the Salt River.

What possible issue was I concerned about? Finding my rider in the many small side streets serving the dorms, classrooms and local bars and restaurants, while dodging the light rail trains in the area started me worrying.

Unfortunately, the rider hadn't turned on the "Share My Location" feature, so all I had was an approximate pickup location. That feature, when activated by the rider creates a little blue stick figure on the driver's screen showing the exact location of the rider's phone.

When I arrived at the designated site, I was not surprised I couldn't identify my rider out of the hundreds of young people milling around. I texted "Charcoal SUV at Mill and University with flashers on."

I waited a bit, and texted "Can you see my car?" I received a response, "No." *That was helpful information there.*

I came back, "Where are you?" Her answer was, "I am in front of the Physics module." *Even less helpful information.* I asked, "Can you turn on the 'Share Location' feature, please?" Long pause then, "I don't know what you are talking about. Just drive to the Physics building!" *Arghh.*

Time to try communicating directly, so I chose the "Call Rider" option. Of course, it went straight to voice mail, "I'm sorry. The subscriber's mailbox is full and cannot accept messages at this time. Goodbye."

When you read about a deranged old man trying to strangle an IT person, it will probably be me.

Back to Susan via text. "That was me trying to call you. Can you pick up when I try again?" I received a fast response, "Sure." When I tried this time, she immediately picked up and said in an obviously sarcastic voice, "Yeah, what?" I explained the situation and told her I was attempting to find exactly where she was so I could pick her up and get her to her destination with as little delay as possible. I asked again if she could supply me with cross streets, an actual street address, or turn on the location indicator so I could find her.

"You know, you are making this so hard," she whined. "Just come to the Physics module, and I am right here."

Patience Powers, take a breath.

"Susan, I attended ASU in the early seventies. Everything has grown so much, I don't know where that building is. Can I help you turn on your location feature?" I requested again.

Her very sharp retort to me was, "You are just stupid. I don't know anything about that. I don't like talking to you. Go away." Which after delivering those words, my screen flashed "Rider Canceled Trip."

Perfect. I drove for 15 minutes to arrive exactly at the spot SHE had input when requesting the ride. I spent another 10 minutes idling in the car while reaching her, only to be insulted, yelled at and then cancelled with no renumeration. I have pity for the next rideshare driver. Oh well.

18 ~ I Have Met God; His Name is Steve

12:45 AM – Sunday morning.

I received a request for a pickup at a Hyatt hotel in North Scottsdale. I arrived to find a couple, late thirties, not glamourous, just normal looking people. They got in and we made introductions (Steve and Isabella), and when I slid the start button, the screen reported the trip would take 35 minutes. That is quite a bit longer than the average, and I asked where I was taking them.

"Waffle House," came Steve's answer. "They have the best steak and eggs anywhere." I asked, "Isn't there one in Scottsdale?" He said they had looked, but this was the only one that came up. Trying to ease the 20 plus minute drive to the west valley, I offered, "Okay, settle in. We have some time together. What brings you to the Valley?"

I heard some snickering between themselves, and Isabella replied, "We had two religious conferences to attend here. We are both speakers."

I said, "That sounds interesting. What topics do you speak on?" She perked up and said, "I speak on the numerous misinterpretations of the Bible on the topic of homosexuality."

Oh boy. Yikes. Why do I ask open ended questions? And, I have half an hour of this to go?

"You see," she continued, "the Bible never said that men should not lay with other men. The correct translation is 'men shall not lay with boys,' thereby outlawing pedophilia, not homosexuality. Since women were routinely having clandestine sex with each other due to the lack of men, they were not addressed."

Really? I don't even understand that line of reasoning. Do something, Bill!

In an effort to change the topic to a more believable one, I quickly asked, "So Steve, what topics do you speak on?"

"I speak about being God on earth."

I replied, "I see. So, you explain to everyone how they can live God-driven lives?"

"No, you misunderstand. I am God."

Oh shit. And I brought it on myself.

Steve continued for at least five miles explaining all the reasons he knew that he was the chosen one, and of his efforts to convince everyone else of that obvious (to him) fact.

Desperately wanting to change the topic off his self-serving sermon I offered, "So Steve, tell me about the steak and eggs that Waffle House has. Why are they so good?"

"I'm not sure," he replied. "They just cook it perfectly. We look for them every time we travel."

I saw the familiar yellow / black letters ahead, and said, "Well here we are," and pulled into the lot. But something was wrong. The lights were on, but everyone was standing outside the door. I pulled up, rolled the window down and asked, "What's up?" A guy walked over and said, "They had a grease fire in the kitchen, and they are waiting for the fire department now."

Shit, and double shit.

The thought of spending another half hour driving Steve and Isabella back to their hotel was unbearable. In the back of my mind, I seemed to remember there was another Waffle House a few miles north just off I-17. I ended their ride on the app and told them of my recollection. "Do you mind if I drive you there and see? You won't be charged for it."

Steve's hunger dictated, "Go for it. We are already on the other side of town. What's a few more miles?"

I silently prayed (not to Steve) that the restaurant was indeed where I remembered. I saw the identical letters ahead, and thanked God (not Steve) for answering my prayer. The lights were on and there were a number of patrons inside. I dropped them off and wished them all the best in their endeavors.

Steve said, "You have been a very attentive driver. Can we buy you a late dinner, and then you can drive us back?"

"Wow," I replied. "That is a very generous offer, but I am tired, and I want to get home to my wife. But thanks anyway."

I tried hard not to spin my tires as I made my escape. I headed back into normality. Thank GOD!

19 ~ The UBER Button

Sometimes, you must improvise when dealing with inebriated passengers. I have explained how I have accessed my "Dad voice" when dealing with unruly young men—and girls sometimes. I have found that voice effective up to mid-thirties riders. The next story will explain how drivers need to think on their feet when presented with something outside the norm.

11:30 PM – Saturday night

I received a request from rider Matthew to pick up in a very high-priced area in Carefree. No gates to deal with, but a very stunning home was attached to the address. I pulled in the gigantic courtyard and notified Matthew through the app that I had arrived. The front doors quickly opened, and three obviously drunk guys stumbled to the car, trying to hide their drinks. When they piled in, I got a hint of the trouble ahead when I said, "Guys, open containers are against the law in every town in the Valley."

"What, are you a cop?" replied Matthew, sitting right beside me up front, and all three of them thought that was hilarious (even thought it was an oft repeated phrase by actor Martin Mull, standup comic, and frequent guest pharmacist on *Two and a Half Men*.)

Trouble.

Against my better judgement, I ignored the drinks and started driving.

I saw the destination was over twenty miles away and I asked, "Where are you guys going that far away?"

"Tits man, tits and ass," came the overly loud response from the back seat.

I'm pushing seventy years old. That language doesn't faze me. It was a perfectly precise answer to my question. They were headed to a topless bar.

"May I ask why you chose that particular establishment? There are several of them closer," I offered.

"We're from Seattle. We were watching the ball game at our rich friend's mansion. We don't know where we are. We just picked one," explained Matthew who was showing himself to be the alpha dog in the car.

He might become the source of the trouble I sensed was brewing.

We were headed south on Cave Creek Blvd., and I suggested, "There is a place not far from here named the Candy Store. I have picked up a few guys from there and I haven't heard any complaints."

I didn't share that I had picked up bartenders and dancers from there after their shifts as well. TMI

"Take us there!" boomed from the back seat.

Have you noticed the more inebriated some people get, the louder their voices become? Based on that criterion, this car is headed for trouble.

That fleeting thought turned into a real possibility when Matthew slurred, "Did I tell you I murdered a guy?"

Here comes the trouble.

"No, and I really don't want to hear about it," I replied, realizing my Dad voice was not going to work with these guys.

I had passed the cop car about a mile before, and I started easing off the gas slightly as I continued speaking to Matthew, purposely raising my voice so the guys in the rear could hear. "Look, I have already pushed the button once. I need you guys to calm down, or I will push it twice."

The constant roar of obscenities and laughing ceased. The alpha dog barked, "What button?"

"Well, there has been a rash of problems that UBER drivers have been reporting with rowdy riders, present company excluded of course."

Excluded my ass.

"UBER has instituted a GPS enabled system that will identify cars with potential problems with a color-coded car ID. We are now in 'Yellow Stage'." As if it was planned, the light ahead turned red.

Perfect.

"This car is now appearing on all their screens as yellow." The Phoenix Police cruiser in the adjacent lane had been slowly gaining on my car and pulled up alongside us at the light. I leaned forward, smiled, and waved at the cop. He smiled and waved back.

Double perfect.

My grandfather used to take me fishing when I was a kid in Oak Creek Canyon in the red rock country of northern Arizona. I chuckled to myself hearing his words, "You have to set the hook." Thanks for the advice, Gramps. Hook set.

The entire environment in the car had changed as we idled at the light. Matthew quietly said, "What happens if you press the button a second time?"

I replied calmly, "Oh, the car will immediately show 'Red Status' and we will be stopped instantly. In this case with your open containers that I warned you about, handcuffs and indictments will probably occur."

"Where is the button?" Matthew asked.

"I'm sorry, I am not allowed to reveal its location," I somehow managed to say with a straight face.

The light changed and the cop car magically stayed by our side right up to the turnoff into the bar. As we started to turn, I waived to the cop, and he laughed and waived back. Thank God for the lighted blue UBER light in my windshield.

Cops actually like us. We cut down on the drunks behind the wheel. Case in point times 3 sitting in my car.

As they were exiting my vehicle, the now quiet beta dog asked, "You won't report us for the open containers, will you?"

My stern reply was, "Not if you deposit them in that trash container by the door. Enjoy your evening."

As I was pulling away, I glanced in the mirror and watched all of them dutifully depositing their drinks in the trash. I knew darn well the bouncer would make them do the same thing, but I smiled at the slight pressure that I had placed on them after the self-described murderer scared the snot out of me. I then started chuckling thinking ahead to when they all arrived back at SeaTac, entered another UBER vehicle, and start asking where the UBER button is. Priceless.

20 ~ Lost but Never Found

When you start driving for UBER, there really isn't a step-by-step procedure manual, or if there is, I never saw it. It was trial by fire. One of the first things I learned was that people leave things in your car. They don't mean to, but somehow, it's the driver's fault if they don't get the item back. After a year or so of dutifully returning those varied items to "UBER Central" in Tempe within a day or so of discovering them, I realized no rider even knew the place existed. It could be because it's called Greenlight Hub. That really doesn't scream "Find your lost stuff here."

I came up with a plan that has worked well for my riders. I give them all a card with my cell number on it. I tell them if they think they left something in my car, they just need to call or text me, and I'll look for it. If I find it, I'll arrange to get it back to them. It sounds simple because it is. Over the years I have returned wallets, purses, phones, keys, credit cards, glasses, gloves, a skateboard, and a hearing aid.

A few years ago, I saw that UBER instituted an online program which in essence tries to accomplish the same thing but convolutes everything. You are not given the driver's cell number but there is a conduit to notify the driver. If you connect with that person, and you arrange to get the item back with the driver, UBER charges a fee.

Unbelievable. What costs did UBER incur? Just have the rider call the driver directly.

I don't understand the problem of simply giving out my cell number. If I truly give five-star service, why would I fear any negativity? All I have ever received is positive feedback. I am sure UBER won't like it because I get direct requests outside the UBER system. I have repeatedly asked UBER why a rider can't simply request a specific driver through the system. The technology is definitely there. Every UBER driver has a unique identifier. Why not let the rider decide who shows up?

Just before this went to press, I received a notice that UBER was beta-testing this very suggestion in San Francisco. If it works there, they will roll it out in other major markets.

Wow. They listened. I am looking forward to having this hit Phoenix. I never really liked going around the parent company, but the customers keep requesting me to pick them or their kids up because they already knew and trusted me.

21 ~ Mask Nazi NOT

Last quarter 2019

The Covid pandemic affected everyone on the planet. I cannot imagine the heartbreak, financial woes, illness, and death that millions of people suffered worldwide. I can only relate how it affected this retired old guy safely driving drunks home in the middle of the night.

Like other people, I first heard about this flu coming out of China around December of 2019. It did not sound that important at the time. As is my habit, I met with my doctor near the end of January for my annual physical. The news had intensified around this possible "pandemic," and I asked him about it. He had been studying it and told me that he was concerned about my ability to fight it.

"Bill, you have had asthma all your life. Your lungs are compromised. Your age comes into play. If you contract this virus and end up in the hospital, your odds are fifty-fifty on getting out alive." ... *Gulp.*

I asked him what was going to happen. He said scientists all over the world will be working on vaccines to combat this virus. He advised me to limit my day-to-day contact with people, especially indoors. He specifically advised me to suspend my UBER driving until a vaccine is developed. So, in November 2019, I completely stopped picking up passengers. I limited my exposure by only doing UberEATS deliveries for over a year.

In December of 2020, Pfizer and Moderna were granted emergency authority to vaccinate first responders with their new 2-dose medications designed to protect humans from contracting the virus.

In January 2021, the category of "Essential Personnel" was added to the list of people eligible for the treatments, and UBER drivers were specifically mentioned.

I received my first Pfizer shot on February 12th and my follow up on March 4th. I have subsequently received the two follow up boosters, and I intend to continue boosting as advised by my doctor. In my opinion, we will all be looking at annual shots just like the flu. Oh well.

So, after waiting the required time after my first shot, I started picking up passengers once again. The world had changed, and UBER did as well. First up, new cleaning and disinfectant procedures daily. We were required to prove that we had our masks on at all times we had passengers in the car. We were forced to take a photo of our face adequately covered at the start of our tour, and again every four hours or so. We were continually ordered to not accept any riders that weren't wearing masks. If they objected, and MANY people did, we were told to drive away.

UBER's requirements, NOT the drivers'.

This five-star driver complied totally for the first few months, but as the growing rift between mask wearers and objectors grew, I started ignoring the mandates and dealt with the people by simply asking questions, instead of ordering compliance.

I started a survey cased on my experience with the Pfizer set vs. the Moderna series that my wife had. I received the first shot in early 2021, and I felt like Mike Tyson had pummeled my left arm. It hung loosely at my side for about a day, and then everything was fine. About a week later, my wife received her first shot, and came back swirling her arm all around. "You are such a wimp," she taunted.

I got my revenge after my second shot produced no pain or bad symptoms at all. Not so for the tough woman I was married to. She was down for days. She said she never remembered feeling so sick.

So, I started asking my riders if they had been vaccinated, and if so, what were their experiences. To my surprise, most of them reported the same results; Pfizer first shot = sore arm, no issues after the second one. Moderna first shot = no issues, and varying levels of sickness after the second one. The Johnson and Johnson single shot came out a few months later, and the results were all over the board.

What I found was the riders were more than happy to participate, and we all learned about this brave new world we had been thrust into, without the conflict.

I have since received two booster shots and it looks like they are going to be handled just like the annual flu shots with new formulas to attack the variants.

22 ~ Mask Politics of a Boy Toy

1:45 PM – Saturday night

I picked up a delightful, mature woman named Margie at an upscale restaurant in Scottdale and set off on a 22-minute drive to the outskirts of Fountain Hills.

The Town of Fountain Hills is a master planned community established in 1970 by McCulloch Properties (now MCO Properties, Inc.). Prior to 1970 the area was a cattle ranch and was part of one of the largest land and cattle holdings in Arizona. The land was purchased by Robert McCulloch in the late 1960s and the community designed by Charles Wood, Jr. (designer of Disneyland in southern California).

The centerpiece of Fountain Hills is the beautiful fountain. It serves as a focal point for the community and attracts thousands of visitors each year.

The fountain was built in 1970 by Robert McCulloch the year before reconstruction of the London Bridge in Lake Havasu City, another of McCulloch's projects. The fountain sprays water for about fifteen minutes every hour at the top of the hour. The plume rises from a concrete water lily sculpture in the center of a large man-made lake. driven by three 600 horsepower turbine pumps, sprays water at a rate of 7,000 gallons per minute though an 18-inch nozzle. With all three pumps and under ideal conditions, the fountain reaches 560 feet in height, though in normal operation only two of the pumps are used, with a fountain height of around 300 feet. When built, it was the world's tallest fountain and held that record for over a decade.

I anticipated a nice drive; however, that was not to be the case. Maggie had a thirty-something boy toy (Bobby) with her. It was the start of the Mandatory Mask era, and I was required by UBER to insist that every passenger was wearing a mask and it had to be worn correctly, mouth and nose covered. Bobby, of course, had his mask defiantly slung under his chin. I was still in the restaurant lot, and after my usual introductions, I said, "Bobby, it's nice to meet you. UBER has strict rules. I can't start driving until all my riders are properly masked."

"That's just stupid! "he whined. "I am an American. I have inalienable rights! I can't be forced to do anything I don't want to do."

I think any UBER driver would tell you that they heard many versions of this tirade during our forced mask regulations.

"Oh, for God's sake, Bobby. You sound like a little child. Bill is simply following the rules. Put your mask on."

Go Maggie!

He grudgingly, slid the mask up and pouted. I thought that was the end of it, but he was just starting. "Who did you vote for? Are you one of those Democrat liberals that are giving away all our rights? Why are you driving for UBER anyway? Couldn't you get a real job?"

Pleasant fellow. I looked at the time to go. 19 minutes. Shit.

It was obvious that he wasn't expecting me to answer because he just kept going. "Trump is right. This Corona thing is a big overblown hoax. It will be over in a month or so and only the real elderly will be dying from it. We in the United States will be shielded from most of this anyway. This vaccination scheme is just a ploy by big pharma to dupe small-minded people to give them money."

I truly wanted to ask him where he received his medical degree, but I kept my mouth shut.

All through this tirade, Maggie had been silent. Was she of the same mind, or did Bobby bring something more to the table other than his brilliant comments? I was betting on the latter.

"So, Maggie," I asked hoping to get off Bobby's radar, "how long have you lived in Fountain Hills?"

"My ex and I had the house built in 2000," she replied. "I got it in the divorce last year."

"And then she jumped in bed with me," Bobby chimed in. "Best swap she has ever made in her life!"

This guy just keeps getting worse.

I glanced at Maggie in the mirror. She grimaced.

We drove the rest of the way with Sinatra on the radio, and after driving up the long meandering street into her courtyard, I remarked on the incredible nighttime vista.

"And she paid for it on her back!" Bobby remarked laughing as he threw his mask into my backseat.

Yikes. Oh well.

I thanked Maggie and headed back into town. I pulled in the first gas station and threw Bobby's discarded mask away.

23 ~ Transient Families

2:15 AM – Saturday morning

I arrived at a Red Roof Inn located in a very sketchy part of town and found the ground floor room indicated on my app. I texted the rider, Nancy, that I had arrived. The door opened immediately, and a family of four started loading up my SUV with luggage, blankets, pillows, and clothes. They seemed to be in a rush.

"If you don't mind me asking, what is going on here?" She said they had a great opportunity to move to a better place. I had to tie down boxes of kitchen utensils to my luggage rack on top. I asked if they were taking anything that didn't belong to them, and they assured me they weren't. It was obvious that they didn't have any money and were just getting by. When we got everything loaded, and everyone belted in (quite the ordeal), the app headed us to a better part of the valley.

As we drove, I asked about the early morning departure, and Nancy said it was the only time she and her husband were together to be able to actually move. They both worked two jobs and couldn't get any time off. Their credit was so bad, they couldn't rent a normal apartment, so they went from one weekly rental hotel to another.

Yikes.

After they got checked in with a bleary-eyed attendant, we started moving them in. I started piling all their worldly possessions onto the courtyard sidewalk as the kids were planning where their stuff would go. I asked them if they had taken time to eat, and they said no, so off I went to Filiberto's and brought back a banquet of Mexican food that we all enjoyed. We finished their move around four, and they attempted to thank me with a tip they couldn't afford. I smiled and told them to use it for something special for the kids.

Time to count my blessings.

24 ~ Drunk Blonde Stalking

12:01 AM – Saturday morning

The Buffalo Chip Saloon is a bar in "downtown" Cave Creek. For anyone who has been there, you will understand the quotes around the area. The saloon is huge with multiple dance floors and is packed weekend nights. Anyway, I received a rider request for a pickup at that bar from rider I'll call Kristi which was 17 minutes away from the north Phoenix restaurant where I had just dropped off two patrons.

I accepted the ride, and as is my custom, texted, "I'm on my way," to the rider. I immediately received a response, "I'm here." I ignored the obvious and continued towards the bar. "I'm here." Came across again about a minute later. Again, I ignored the text. Where else would she be but at my pickup point? "I'm here," came in a third time. Okay, I get it. She's drunk.

I pulled over to text, "7 minutes out," and continued onward. "I'm here."

Arggh, get over it, Bill. You deal with drunks every weekend.

I received two more identical texts before I arrived at the bar. I pulled up to the front door, turned my flashers on and texted my rider "I've arrived. Charcoal SUV. Flashers on."

The front porch was packed and when no one looked my way, I started scanning the completely full parking lot. She was easy to spot. 5'6", blonde, barely wearing a halter top, short cut-offs, phone glued in front of her face, and stumbling back and forth at the edge of the lot.

"Are you Kristi?" I yelled over the music and roar of the revelers.

She waived and stumbled to my car. "Are you my UBER driver, Bill? What took you so long? I've been waiting over an hour!" she exclaimed, all in one breath and huffed as she dropped into the back seat.

Before I could point out that she requested the ride only 17 minutes prior, she continued, "Can you believe they threw me out of the bar? They did it to me last week too! Why do they keep doing it?"

I had a pretty good idea, but I just asked her to belt in, and we started off on what was supposed to be a 21-minute drive.

Sounds like the theme song from Gilligan's Island ... and actually a good metaphor for what was about to transpire.

About four minutes into the drive as we rounded the corner just leaving the "downtown" strip, she shouted, "Wait, you missed my salon!"

What salon? She hadn't mentioned a salon.

"What salon?" I asked evenly.

"My hair salon. It's back there. I need to pick up some makeup."

I slowed for a U-turn and started back towards the bar. "Which side of the street is it on?" I asked. "It's on the left side of the street. It's before the Circle K." I think I have mentioned this before, but Cave Creek doesn't believe in streetlights, so we were driving very slowly as she searched for her place of business. All the time she is literally hanging out the window saying, "Just a little further."

I was eyeing the Circle K coming up on the left. As we passed the store, she said, "Oh, never mind, I don't need it. Just take me home." Gladly. I executed another U-turn and headed back towards north Phoenix.

As we were approaching Carefree Highway, the street made famous by Gordon Lightfoot, Kristi screams, "Oh my God! Jenny has my keys. I can't get into my house!"

Who is Jenny, and why do I think another U-turn is about to happen?

"Jenny is my girlfriend. They didn't throw her out of the bar. She is still back there and has my keys."

As I turned around again, I instructed, "Please call Jenny and tell her we are on our way back to the bar, and to meet you at the front door with your keys."

As I retraced our path for the third time, she said, "Jenny is not answering her phone." I continued driving back to the bar and instructed her to text Jenny as well, hoping she would notice that more than a ring over the din of the country music.

We arrived back at the bar a little after 1a.m.. I parked in the same no parking zone with my blue UBER light and flashers going. I turned around and quickly assessed that Kristi was in no shape to find Jenny in the massive crowd inside the saloon. And that would be if the bouncers would let her back in anyway.

"What does Jenny look like?" I asked, thinking that by some grace of God I can find her in the crowd of almost 2,000.

"Well, she's about my height, skinny, absolutely no tits, brunette, and she has tattoos all down one arm." That last bit of information gave me some hope, so I said, "Kristi, STAY IN THE CAR. I will go try to find Jenny and get your keys. DON'T TOUCH ANYTHING. I'll be back."

The last instructions were from years of dealing with inebriated people. You must revert back to child level discussions.

I didn't foresee that I would have any problems simply entering the place, look around for Jenny and retrieve Kristi's keys. I was wrong on so many levels starting with the twenty-something bouncer at the front door.

He wanted a cover charge. My Dad voice ended that nonsense with, "You folks just threw out the drunk blonde who is in the back seat of my car. If I don't go in and retrieve her keys so she can get in her house, I will call the Maricopa County Sherriff and have them come down, close the club to search for her girlfriend to retrieve her keys."

Total bullshit, but delivered with the aforementioned deep voice, and the kid folded.

"I'm sorry sir. Let me put a wristband on you so you won't have any further problems." The other security person was a young lady who had tattoos down one arm.

Oh, no. That is not an encouraging sign.

She laughed and wished me luck. I proceeded into the dark, crowded and very noisy dance hall. I started asking every brunette with tattoos down one arm if she was Jenny.

I received the expected response of "No" until about the tenth girl. Her response was to lean towards me suggestively and she whispered, "I could be Jenny tonight."

Oh shit.

"No, I'm sorry, I am looking for Jenny who has her girlfriend's house keys." I stammered.

"I have keys," she said with the same flirtatious voice.

Double shit.

"Thanks. Maybe some other time. I need to keep looking. Sorry."

I then exited the interior and surveyed the huge back patio. There were more people here than inside. This is crazy. I had been gone from the car for at least fifteen minutes, and the chances of me finding Jenny were non-existent.

I grabbed another security kid, asked if he had 86'ed a blonde earlier. He said he hadn't, but to ask the head of security if he could help. "He's the old guy wearing the cowboy hat," pointing to a 40-ish man.

Sheesh. Old man? I had 30 years on him. Oh well.

I walked up, explained my dilemma to him, and he laughed. "So, you are an UBER driver that has a drunk blonde that we tossed in your back seat, and you are trying to find another drunk tattooed brunette in this crowd to get your rider's house keys?

You know, when I heard it spelled out like that, I realized who the crazy person was.

He said, "You know, if I were you, I would get her home and drop her in front and drive away as fast as I could."

Sage advice.

I thanked him and hurried back to the car. I was relieved to see it was still where I left it, and even better, my passenger was passed out in the back.

As I left the bar, I glanced at the dash clock. After 1:30 a.m.! Well, at least I will enjoy a quiet drive to her house. I'll cross the bridge of getting her inside when we arrive.

"Is that Frank Sinatra?" she shouted scaring the snot out of me. I had the satellite radio on low. "I love Sinatra. Can you play 'My Way'?"

"Sorry, this is the Sinatra channel. I can't select a specific song. It's just whatever the playlist is." I explained to the drunk person who I just knew didn't understand what I just tried to explain.

My assessment was confirmed when she shouted, "Alexa, play 'My Way'!" She repeated the command twice more before I interrupted with, "Kristi, I don't have Alexa in my car. Your requests won't do anything."

She settled back and then leaned forward and said, "I'm hungry. Will you stop at McDonalds please?" I replied, "Kristi, McDonalds is closed." "No, they're not. The one by my house is open 24-hours. It's right ahead under the overpass."

I knew the one she was referring to. It was one of the express versions inside a Shell station convenience store. I was pretty sure it was closed but acquiesced and drove there. I saw it was indeed closed. I pointed out the outdoor signs were not lit, and you could see the roll down gate between the restaurant and store was closed. Despite my protests, she got out of the car and staggered to the door.

You get used to assessing the area you find yourself stopped in around 1:30 in the morning. I looked around for anyone paying attention to the young blonde girl who was obviously drunk going into the store, and my eyes fell on a homeless looking guy in the shadows of an adjacent building. I kept my eyes split between watching him and my rider shaking the roll down gate inside the store.

Am I ever going to be done with this ride?

Kristi eventually stumbled our carrying a bag of jerky and got back into the rear seat. I kept my eyes on the transient as I exited the lot and waited for the light to turn left and finish this marathon trip.

I noticed the car for the first time when it ran the light behind us coming from the Shell station that we had just left.

Hmm. Possibly an unmarked cop keeping an eye on the drunk woman in the UBER vehicle. Maybe.

I waited at the light under the overpass and turned left to catch the frontage road. Yep, the car ran the same light I had just gone through and followed at a distance onto the frontage road. I was now coming up on her street, which was completely residential. I turned right and kept my eye in the rearview mirror. On schedule, the car turned right and slowed to a stop about three houses behind us.

"Kristi, STAY IN THE CAR. I need to check on something." I instructed. I got out of the car and started walking towards what I thought would be a cop, and immediately the car swerved into a tight U-turn. The only noise I heard was screeching tires. My brain registered a few things instantly. Not a cop. Prius. Damn that car could move. Driver looked like Mr. Spacely on the Jetson's. Out of state plate. I tried to get the license number, but my 70-year-old eyes aren't as good as they used to be. Wow. That guy was definitely out for no good.

I returned to my car, opened the rear door, and attempted to explain to Kristi what just happened. She had just been stalked.

"Oh, I'm sure that you're wrong. It was probably one of my neighbors. Everyone is nice here." I attempted a few more times to convince her we should file a report. "What if this guy comes back after I leave?" I pleaded.

She was adamant. "I don't want to call the cops."

"How are you going to get in your house without keys?" I asked.

"I don't know. I'll find a way," she said as she staggered to her front door.

I wasn't going anywhere until she got inside.

I watched as she gave up on the front door, then moved to the code pad on the garage. She obviously couldn't remember her code, so she proceeded to stumble around to the side yard. It was completely dark back there, but I could see her lit phone screen as it wobbled at shoulder level, then drop to waist high, and then drop to the ground.

Shit.

I went back to my car, grabbed my flashlight, and walked around the corner to find her sitting with her back against the house. She squinted against the flashlight's glare and whined, "I can't open the gate." I helped her to her feet, reached over the fence and unlatched to gate. She slid in and shut it. I asked her through the fence how she was going to get in her house. "Oh, I have a key hidden by the back door."

At that second, the stalker was the least of her physical safety issues. I could have gladly strangled her for all the nonsense over the past two hours of nonsense.

I simply wished her a good night and returned to my car. I waited until I watched the interior lights start coming on. I signed her out, and as I drove away my UBER screen notified me that my whopping fare of $28 was credited to my GoBank account. I could have made more flipping burgers for the same 2 hours of effort. The funny thing about all of that was she will probably remember very little of her adventures, especially being in the VERY real danger she was in.

25 ~ Semper Fi

4:15 AM – Saturday morning

I was heading home after an exceptionally long Friday night of picking up drunks, and I was looking forward to a great breakfast and a nap. I don't know why I went online for one more drive, but I did, and it immediately beeped and instructed me to pick up Dave at Terminal 4.

No problem, or so I thought.

This was very early in my driving career, and I was not completely sure of airport protocol, but I lived here all my life and had been in and out of Sky Harbor hundreds of times, so when I saw American Airlines, I headed for the arrival lanes and pulled up in front of baggage claim and notified my rider that I had arrived. As I was texting the color of my SUV to Dave, a big guy in a florescent vest rapped on my window.

"Are you UBER?" he barked.

I resisted the urge to point to the lighted sign in the windshield and simply said, "Yes, sir."

"Well, you just cost yourself $245.00."

"Why," I croaked.

"Because you rideshare vehicles are prohibited from using the interior lanes to pick up riders. You need to use the outside lane."

"I'm sorry, sir," I responded. "I am new at this. I'll make sure that I will do that next time."

I can grovel when needed.

"Too late," he chastised and started towards the rear of my car. I started texting Dave that I would be a few minutes more when the vest guy walks back to my window and asked, "Are you a Marine?"

I had forgotten the Marine plate on my car. I answered, "No, sir. My son was (or is. *Once a Marine* and all that). Iraq. He is retired now.

I keep the plate on the car because the families of fallen Marines receive the license proceeds."

"Well, Semper Fi," he said as he tore the ticket up. "It's a good thing you got a jarhead here first. These other dweebs would have written you up for sure. Thank you for your son's service!"

I asked, "Should I drive around the terminal and come back into the outside lane?" He replied, "Hang on. Can you reach your rider and see where he is?" he asked.

"Sure, just let me use the system and I'll get him on the phone." I did, and when Dave answered, I said "Dave, this is your UBER driver, Bill. Can you tell me where you are?" He said, "Sure, we are right here in the rideshare pickup area on the outer curb."

Ouch.

"Is that you with the traffic cop?" The vest and I looked over to where I should have been, and they were waving. I said to the vest, "I appreciate what you just did. I'll loop around the terminal and come back into the outside lane."

He stopped me. "Hang on. I'll fix this." He proceeded to stop all the lanes of traffic and wave Dave and his family across to my car. He continued guiding traffic around my car as I loaded their luggage. As I closed the hatch, I turned, shook his hand, and I said, "Semper Fi." He smiled and waved as we departed.

Dave said, "Wow. That was impressive. We never had an UBER driver with that kind of clout before."

Semper Fi, indeed.

26 ~ Visiting the Real Tent City

In the early nineties, then Maricopa County Sheriff, Joe Arpaio, came on the scene and started a controversial reign of *innovative ideas* such as pink underwear, black and white striped inmate uniforms, green baloney, and his most audacious project, Tent City.

Most residents were appalled that he would house county jail inmates in Army Korean-era surplus tents in the hottest city in the country. Critics called it the "Phoenix Concentration Camp." Arpaio said it was just part of his get-tough approach that gained him fame as "America's Toughest Sheriff" by Penthouse Magazine. It was eventually torn down by Arpaio's successor as cruel and unusual punishment. Tent City cost taxpayers about $8.6 million the last year it was open. Officials in April said closing the facility would save approximately $4.5 million annually. This is a story about the true tent city of Phoenix that continues to exist today.

As of the date of this printing, Phoenix has renamed this area The Zone, and is relocating people to downtown motels that it has purchased.

1:15 AM – Saturday

Heading for an address on McDowell Avenue in east Phoenix, I slowed but passed the correct entrance for an apartment building. I turned into the adjoining complex and had to drive around to the back to reverse course. There was a chain link fence separating the two medium-sized properties, and I saw a middle-aged woman unloading items from inside her car. On a hunch I asked, "Are you Millie?" She replied, "Well yes, I am. How did you know that?" I explained that I was her UBER driver who missed the turn, and she said, "Oh that's okay. I miss the addresses all the time. Can you come around and help me?"

I already like this woman.

"No problem. I'll be right over," and I came around to the right complex. She had a number of bags on the ground, and I loaded them up in the back. She shut the doors to her car and hopped in the back of mine. My curiosity of why she had called for and UBER driver when she had her own transportation was answered when she said, "Good riddance. The Lord has decided I don't need a car!"

"How so?" I asked.

"The car started making bad noises and smoking really badly. It died in the street, and God sent a few wonderful men to push it into this apartment parking lot. I was just moving all the stuff out of the car because somebody will be towing it away soon. I can't afford it anyway."

I really like this woman.

I started driving towards an address I recognized as a run-down part of old downtown Phoenix. Millie complimented me on how nice my car was, and generally kept up a good-natured conversation as we drove. We passed the Diamondbacks' and Suns' stadiums and headed south on 15th Avenue. I hadn't been in this part of town in decades and was shocked at what it had become. Where warehouses and low-priced office and retail space used to be, there were now vacant lots occupied by all kinds of camping tents, pickup truck camper shells (sans truck), and some cardboard lean-tos.

She directed me to pull over to the curb, and I helped her unload all her car contents on the sidewalk. I asked if I could help her move her stuff off the sidewalk to wherever she was staying, and she looked at me smiling.

"You know, most UBER drivers won't even come down here, let alone offer to help us with our stuff."

I really didn't know what to say, so I started picking up the larger items and said, "Where to, Millie?"

Even though it was now after two in the morning, as we walked towards her destination, wherever that was, she stopped at three separate tents. She softly called out at each one, and when the occupant stuck their head out Millie would hand different packages or bags to them. She would receive an immediate smile and thanks for whatever groceries or small items they needed. We went back and forth to the sidewalk until all the items had been delivered. This had been a charity delivery all the time.

I was humbled by her efforts.

She said, "Can you take me home, or do I need to get another driver out here?"

"Millie, it would be my honor to take you home. Where are we going?" She gave me an address not too far from our present location, but definitely in a better part of town. She explained that a number of the occupants of this tent city were parishioners of her church that had fallen on hard times. She had taken upon herself to help them as best she could. I asked her when she was going to get her car fixed, and if I can take her to pick it up.

She said, "Bill, I told you. The Lord has decided that car is no longer in my life. I will get by without it." We pulled up to a small apartment building and she said, "I want to thank you so much for all your help tonight. How much do I owe you?" I answered, "Not a dime, Millie. I think the Lord put me here to help you as well."

She smiled a huge smile and said, "Bless you, Bill. You will be rewarded in heaven, but here is something for your gas." She produced a wad of crumpled ones and pressed them in my hand despite my sincere objections.

As I drove away, I found that Millie's very presence in my car had uplifted me. It put me in a good mood even though I was headed to pick up at least one more belligerent drunk tonight.

27 ~ Dad's Death

Early Christmas Day in 1975, my phone startled me out of a sound sleep. It was my mom, and she was crying. She simply said, "I have some horrible news. Dad is dead."

Since her father had been in and out of the hospital, was in ill health, constantly in pain, and was well into his nineties, I assumed that was who she was referring to. I comforted her by offering, "Mom, he lived a long life, and he touched many people during his time on Earth. I am sure he is not hurting anymore."

"Are you drunk?" my mother shouted. "I'm talking about YOUR dad!" She haltingly related the previous two hours of hell. My dad was struck by a car that careened around the turn at Central and Missouri as he was putting the key in the car door to open it. "Can you come to Good Samaritan Hospital right away?" she pleaded. In shock, I mumbled that I would be right there.

My house was just blocks away from the church, and I didn't hesitate to head directly there to see where my father was killed. The entire intersection was closed with police cars, traffic cones and flares burning bright directing traffic around the crime scene. I hardly slowed down as I ran over cones and a flare to stop my car about fifty feet from my dad's car.

I hadn't even had a chance to grab the door handle when a cop not much older than me yanked the door open with his hand on his gun and barked, "What the hell do you think you are doing?" He looked like he was ready to shoot. I looked him in the eyes and said, "I came to see where my father was killed."

The cop folded. His angry demeanor dissolved instantly, and he asked quietly, "What is your name?"

I responded, "Bill Powers. My dad's name is Jim Powers."

He started waving the numerous officers running our way mouthing, "He's the son."

Everyone instantly calmed down and came over to offer their condolences. The first cop asked, "What do you need to know?" I asked him to walk me through what happened, and he led me to the car. As we slowly approached the spot where my father left this Earth, he related what he had gathered.

There was a well-maintained bridle path where riders would walk their horses in good weather. It also served as an overflow parking area for the church. My dad's car was parked well off the shoulder between two towering palm trees.

The driver was heading east on Missouri Avenue at a high rate of speed. He attempted to turn north on Central Avenue and swung wide across two lanes and into the dirt shoulder. He brushed my brother-in-law who was carrying my infant niece waiting for the locks to open, and then slammed into my dad's body. My dad (and the car door) were thrown approximately 100 feet. The car continued speeding north on Central Avenue and was gone before anyone could stop it.

There were quite a few witnesses coming out of the church and they described a white Mustang with a young man at the wheel. Out of state plates were recorded by more than one witness. The young cop walked me back to my car and said, "We will find the guy who did this." I thanked him and continued to the hospital.

My mom was a wreck. I asked my brother-in-law Pat if he was okay. He related that he saw the car a moment before and jumped up. The car spun him around and he dropped the car seat with my niece in it, but both were fine. My mom and sister were on the opposite side of the car and watched the whole event unfold in a split second. They were both a little unhinged.

I went over, sat down and held my mom's hand. She related what I had already been told, and between sobs asked, "I need you to do some things for me."

I replied, "Sure, Mom. Anything."

"They are asking me to identify Jim's body. I can't do it. Can you?"

Shit.

I hesitantly said, "Yes, Mom."

"I also need you to tell his parents in the morning."

Shit, shit, shit.

"Do you mean you haven't called them?" I asked incredulously.

"No, I didn't want to disturb their sleep.

Like you did to me?

"You are picking them up at 8 a.m. as usual for the Christmas morning get together at the house. You can tell them then."

I didn't want to become an orphan by strangling my mother on the spot, so I dutifully replied, "I will take care of it."

The front page of the Arizona Republic carried an article entitled, "Man Killed By Hit And Run Driver." Fortunately, no names were mentioned, but a description of the suspect's car was there. I noticed the unread paper on my grandparent's kitchen table when they ushered me into their apartment. They were all excited about getting to my parent's house to see the grandkids, like me, and know their first great-granddaughter. This was an annual event that had been happening for years, and unfortunately this one would be anything but merry.

"Can we sit down for a second?" I asked. "I've got to tell you something." I honestly don't remember my exact words that I used to inform them their only child was killed just a few hours before, but I do remember the pain. I had never seen my grandfather cry, but I did that morning. We all were doing it.

Looking back on that morning, I think that was the day I became the patriarch of our family.

I asked them if they wanted to forgo the trip to Mom's house, but they said they wanted to go anyway. I took them there, and the entire family, minus one, spent that Christmas morning talking about dad.

As I have related previously, an off-duty cop visiting his girlfriend spotted the car in the parking lot about a week later, and they arrested a 19-year-old out of state kid. The trial was a few months later. I learned the hard way the arguments of probative evidence versus prejudicial evidence. The fact that this kid was on probation in another state for killing a woman while driving drunk was NOT admitted into the trial. He received ANOTHER probation in Arizona for killing my dad. Two human beings dead, and the kid (now man) is still driving (unless he killed himself or another person driving under the influence).

Law sucks sometimes.

My dad's father died within a year. Almost everyone in our family knew he died from a broken heart. My grandmother was a tough lady and lived long enough to hold my first-born in her arms. She decreed that I was the person to ensure all of our family members memorials were handled correctly. She had purchased ten burial plots when dad was killed and—unbeknownst to me—put them in my name. "Billy, you are responsible for our entire clan," she announced.

Great. 23 years old and I owned 10 grave sites. Shit. So far, I have buried Dad, Grandpa, Grandma, and my mother. The rest of my very large family have told me they want to be cremated—including me. I sold the rest of the plots. I visit them on Christmas Day every year to honor the day my dad was killed by the drunk driver.

And that is why I drive weekend nights, hopefully fending off any further tragedies. Thanks for reading. Stay safe.

- Bill

Phoenix
Valley of the Sun

Valley of the Sun Statistics

The Phoenix Metropolitan Area—also the Valley of the Sun, the Salt River Valley, or Metro Phoenix and known by most locals simply as "the Valley"—is one of the largest metropolitan areas in the United States. Centered on the city of Phoenix, that includes much of the central part of Arizona. The United States Office of Management and Budget designates the area as the Phoenix-Mesa-Scottsdale Metropolitan Statistical Area (MSA), defining it as Maricopa and Pinal counties. As of the 2020 census, Metro Phoenix had 4,845,832 residents, making it the 11th largest metropolitan area in the nation by population.

Cities, towns, and areas in the Valley of the Sun:

Anthem
Apache Junction
Avondale
Black Canyon City
Carefree
Cave Creek
Chandler
Desert Hills
El Mirage
Estrella
Fountain Hills
Gilbert
Glendale
Gold Canyon
Goodyear
Guadalupe
Litchfield Park
Luke Air Force Base
Mesa

New River
Paradise Valley
Peoria
Rio Verde
Scottsdale
Sun City
Surprise
Tempe

Native American Reservations:

Fort McDowell Yavapai Nation
Gila River Indian Community
Salt River Pima-Maricopa Indian Community
Tohono O'odham Nation

Municipal Airports in the Valley:

Phoenix Sky Harbor (PHX)
Phoenix-Mesa Gateway Airport (AZA)
Scottsdale Airport (SCF)
Deer Valley Airport (DVT)
Falcon Field (MSC)
Phoenix Goodyear Airport (GYR)
Chandler (CHD)
Glendale Airport (GEU)
Buckeye Airport (BXK)

Riders' Remarks

Great Conversation:

Friendly and Fun personality. He made the ride go by super quick with all his stories and jokes. Fun guy to ride with. Highly recommend him!

Great personality and very kind.

Great guy.

My favorite UBER driver. Glad I got to ride with you again.

Thank you, Bill. You made my night. So entertaining and good energy.

Most enjoyable ride ever!

Best convos ever.

Very great and patient driver. He actually got out of his car to find me. Went over and beyond. Great driver all around. Thanks Bill!

Excellent Service:

Above and beyond!

It's been a long time since I have had my door opened for me.

He grabbed my luggage and loaded everything up.

He is always available. I don't know when he sleeps.

All Star Driver

He has driven all our friends. Everyone knows his number.

Dependable!

Late Night Hero:

Bill beat AAA tow truck. He waited with me for them to arrive. I felt completely safe.

He drove me to the gas station, then took me back to my car, and actually showed me how to use the spout lack on the gas can that I had just bought.

Entertaining Driver:

We laughed all the way. He had so many hilarious stories. He MUST write a book!

Acknowledgements

There are so many people to thank for the actual preparation of this book. I am sure I will forget someone and let me apologize for any omissions right up front.

Thanks must go to the hundreds of fun, albeit inebriated, riders that asked the question, "So, what is the craziest thing that has happened driving people home?" After I related a few of the adventures that you have already enjoyed, the constant response was, "You MUST write a book, and we'll buy it!"

Thanks to my darling suffering wife, who has listened to—and watched—countless reiterations of the nightly craziness, until she ordered me to quit talking about them and WRITE A BOOK!

A special thanks to Tailgaters, a Cave Creek sports bar about a mile from my home that had a spot at the end of the bar that became my writer's corner. I spent many lunches and consumed gallons of iced tea there listening to the banter of the regulars, trading affable insults, and earning their interest in my book. Manager Abe, bartenders Courtney, Kristen, April, Lolo, Mo and Mason (who never hesitated to call me when there was a patron who should not be driving themselves home). Which leads me to my final acknowledgements.

Thank you to the following friends of Tailgaters that proofed every chapter you have read. They are, in no particular order:

Jerry Nelson	Doug Rawlings
Phil Trapani	Greg Seybold
Larry Chambers	Joel Coval
Terry Wright	Tim Green

And special thanks to my next-door neighbor Gary McCarthy who is an author of over 30 novels, and who has read every word of this book. He offered great suggestions and was instrumental in getting it published.

Please drive safely.

About the Author

Bill earned his Arizona Real Estate Sales license in 1974, and his Broker's License in 1977. He was the Designated Broker for Homebrokers, a company he founded with an equal partner, Mark Moskowitz. In 1981, he brought a number of agents over to Realty Executives of Phoenix. In 1988, he took over the daunting job of growing the company through franchising. During his tenure, the company grew exponentially, reaching the pinnacle of 880 offices in eight countries with over 19,000 sales agents.

When Bill finally retired in 2011, he spent a year playing dismal golf and passable tennis but wanted to do something more. Remembering his father's death, he chose to spend his time preventing such occurrences by becoming an UBER driver and taking inebriated passengers safely from bars and restaurants to their homes, always offering to pick them up the next day to take them back to pick up their cars at no charge.

Thousands of trips later, he has chronicled some of the most memorable excursions in his first book *UBER @ 2AM*. He is working on a second book with more humorous events occurring in the night and early morning hours in the Valley of the Sun.

I hope you enjoyed the ride along through the Valley of the Sun. Reviews are very important for future sales. If you purchased a book at one of my book signings, Amazon will not be sending you a request for a review. And trying to step through the number of screens to get to the review page can be daunting. No worries! If you aim your phone camera at the QR code below, you will bypass all the steps.

SCAN ME

Note: If you do not have an Amazon account, you will be asked to join. There is no cost to do so. If you have any problems, please reach out to me, I sincerely appreciate all your support. Thanks for reading my first book.

Made in United States
North Haven, CT
27 July 2023

39605246R00049